The S ERDIN

By Douglas V. Jones

From Sleepy Hamlet to Thriving Suburb

Lingering rusticity — Braggington's fields, Erdington June 1931

PUBLISHED BY

Westwood Press Publications

44 BOLDMERE ROAD, SUTTON COLDFIELD
WEST MIDLANDS B73 5TD   TELEPHONE: 0121-354 5913

1

Acknowledgments

The author and publisher wish to thank Birmingham Central Library, Local Studies Department; Mr E. H. Sargeant; Mr. D.A. Spinks and Mr. John Marks for their help in lending photographs and old post-cards. Many of the photographs are from the Benjamin Stone Collection, and several are by the author, Douglas V. Jones. They are also grateful to Birmingham Central Statistical Office for the census statistics quoted in Chapter V.

Sutton for mutton,
Tamworth for beef,
Yenton for a pretty girl
And Brummagem for a thief.

Old couplet, origin unknown

Front cover picture:
The parish church and 'The Green Man', later 'The Acorn',
from an oil painting by an unknown artist

© Copyright

ISBN 0 948025 05 0

First Edition October 1985
2nd Impression Autumn 1987
3rd Impression December 1989
4th Impression January 1993
5th Impression Summer 1995

Printed and Published by The Westwood Press, 44 Boldmere Road Sutton Coldfield, West Midlands. Produced by Offset Litho.

Contents

Station Road, Erdington, June 1926

Wood End Lane, 1925

Erdington Market, June 1929

Introduction

CURIOSITY ABOUT THE ORIGINS of their immediate surroundings attract many people to the study of local history. They pursue the subject, not in the hope of gaining academic distinction, but for the pure love of it, fostered by an insatiable urge to know why things are as they are. In his *Introduction to the Study of History,* V. H. Galbraith goes to the heart of the matter by declaring:

> "The starting point of all enquiry is our immediate environment — the town, the street, the very house in which we live, and the family to which we belong. All these are physical survivals of the past, inviting investigation and linking us with our forefathers."

Events like the coming of the Romans, the Norman Conquest, the Wars of the Roses, the Black Death and the English Civil War all appear in a new and vivid light when we discover their influence on our own town or village.

Erdington, a largely built-up area, leaves little scope for archaeological research, and it has singularly few old buildings. Neither can it boast of great events within its boundaries, and few of its worthies will be found in the pages of the history books. Nevertheless there is a story to be told, the scope for study is wide and the sources of knowledge are varied. In Birmingham there is a first-rate Local Studies Department at the Central Library, and without going further afield the student will find there a wealth of manuscripts and documents; census returns; old photographs; newspaper cuttings and other helpful material.

This short book is intended to demonstrate the amount of history to be found close at hand and to encourage would-be students to pursue the subject further with the prospect of adding to our cumulative knowledge.

Douglas V. Jones

Views from the top of the parish church tower
(Benjamin Stone)

(i) looking north

(ii) looking south

CHAPTER I

Origins

Aston church, with its tall spire and almost the spaciousness of a cathedral, contains effigies of ancient knights and their ladies, over tombs bearing such famous family names as Arden, Holte and Devereux. Here lie Sir Thomas Holte who built nearby Aston Hall, and Sir Edward Devereux, to whom we are indebted for Castle Bromwich Hall. An unknown knight, clad in 15th century plate armour, is commemorated in a mutilated sandstone effigy, discovered under the floor of the church over a century ago. Here, too, in their own chancel, lie members of the family who for several centuries occupied the manor house known as Erdington Hall. The Erdington Chancel, is dominated by the great tomb of Sir Thomas de Erdington, whose sculptured head rests on a helmet, and at his feet crouches a lion. He died in 1433.

Why, we may ask, is there so much emphasis on Erdington in Aston Parish Church? The answer is simple, for, writing of Aston, Sir William Dugdale tells us in his monumental *Antiquities of Warwickshire,* (1656):

"This is a very large parish, and containeth divers hamlets and places of note, including Nechells, Duddeston, Deritend, Bordesley, Heybarnes, Saltley, Ward End, Castle Bromwich, Park Hall and Water Orton, all lying on the south side of Tame, with Witton and Erdington on the north."

There we have it: Erdington was once a tiny hamlet within the phenomenally large parish of Aston.

Erdington Hall, protected on three sides by a double moat and on the fourth by the River Tame, stood on a promontory just south of what is now the junction of Wheelwright Road and Tyburn Road. It was sufficiently near the river to enjoy its protection, but not so near as to be ravished by seasonal flooding. The protection would more likely have been against cattle raiders than sustained military attack. The hall's double moat, which was fed by a small stream rising in the vicinity of Kingsbury Road, survived

Erdington Hall

(Benjamin Stone)

until the 18th century, when it was drained by Sir Charles Holte. The original hall was knocked down before that time — probably in the 17th century. It was replaced by a building on the site which survived until circa. 1912, when it was partially demolished prior to the making of Tyburn Road, with some part of it still surviving until after the first World War. An unknown scribe, writing in 1900, tells us that:

"The remains of the moat still gird the house, here dry and partly choked, there a fine, broad duck-pond . . . The old drawbridge has given place to a more substantial approach, one of the piers of which is flanked by an old mounting-block.

. . . The garden, with its tangled copse; its lawn of long, lush grass; its high bricked walls; its hedge of well-grown hazels; its clustered ferns and flowers; half-wild, half-cultured, is reminiscent of other and, perhaps, happier days."

Double moats, such as the one at Erdington Hall, usually denoted manorial establishments, while single moats often marked the homes of free under-tenants. There were several single moated sites in Erdington. One was near Fern Road; there was another close to the present junction of Moor End Lane and Berkswell Road; and a third once surrounded a farmstead called Pipe Orchard, the site of which can be seen in the playing fields of Erdington Grammar School.

Erdington remained a part of Aston until 1894, in which year it became an urban district with its administrative offices at the Rookery in Kingsbury Road — sometimes referred to as Erdington Council House — the grounds of which are now Rookery Park. In 1911 both Aston Manor and Erdington U.D.C. were absorbed by their huge and expanding neighbour, Birmingham.

Returning to Dugdale on the subject of Aston, he continues by saying:

"It is now commonly called Aston-juxta-Birmingham, but anciently it was written Estone, having originally had that name, perhaps, from the situation thereof, eastwards from Wednesbury in Staffordshire, a town of some note in Saxon times."

Aston belonged to Edwin, Earl of Mercia, before the Conquest, and was bestowed on William Fitz-Ausculf by William I. Its importance at the time of the Domesday survey was reflected in it being rated at eight hides — the same as Sutton — while Birmingham was then only rated at four hides. A

*This ancient hostelry in Bromford Lane
is Erdington's oldest building*

hide represented a variable amount of cultivated land, but was, on average, about 120 acres. It had a church, a mill, which stood near Salford Bridge on the Tame, and woods three miles long and ½ a mile in breadth, all held by a man named Godmund from the Norman overlord.

Let us now turn again to Erdington and consider its name. It may, originally, have been Earda's tun — a 'tun' or 'ton' being a fortified homestead or farm — which in time generally grew into a village or town. Isaac Taylor, in his authoritative book: *Words and Places,* comments: "The suffix 'ton' constitutes a sort of test-word by which we are enabled to discriminate the Anglo-Saxon settlements. It is the most common termination of English local names" and he goes on to say "In most cases the isolated 'ton' became the nucleus of a village, and the village grew into a town."

In the case of Earda — a shortened form of Eardwulf — his 'tun' or fortified homestead, it may be inferred, grew into the imposing house at Bromford, known as Erdington Hall. Dugdale has a different derivation of Erdington's name. "As for the name" he says "I am of the opinion that it originally proceeded from some ancient possessor of it in Saxon times, perhaps Harding, for in the Domesday Book it is written Hardintone''. Then there is the possibility of the name having been at some stage 'Ardington', suggesting a homestead in Arden, (i.e. the Forest of Arden.) Finally, there is the current 'Yenton', a possible corruption of 'Yerdington', a yard or enclosure, which might apply to a moated homestead.

Erdington's early inhabitants have been claimed as river people or "Tame dwellers", who reached the district by following the course of that river from Tamworth in the ninth or tenth centuries. Other nearby river-bank settlements were at Minworth and Curdworth. Some historians think that early settlements were made here by men who came along that ancient, pre-Roman track, once called the Ridgeway, and now the Chester Road. The name 'Ridgeway' is significant, indicating, as it does, a pathway along high or ridged land, a route chosen because it would be less likely to become water-logged in wet weather. This road follows a straight course for much of its way from Coleshill to Brownhills, said to be so because, passing through common-land, it did not have to deviate to avoid privately owned land.

By whatever means Erdington was first colonized, it is worth noting that development of the village centre took place more than a mile to the north of the

Bromford Lane in quieter times

11

riverside settlement and a slightly lesser distance from the Ridgeway. At the time of the Conquest, Erdington, as part of Mercia, belonged to Edwin, Earl of Mercia — grandson of Lady Godiva of Coventry. Edwin appears to have been a courageous man, who resisted the Norman usurpers. As a consequence, he was put to death in 1071, and the earldom then passed to the Crown in the person of William I. The king placed the manor of Erdington, with other manors in the district, in the hands of the aforementioned William Fitz-Ausculf, a powerful Norman baron, who lived in Dudley Castle. He in turn apportioned the manor of Erdington to a man called Peter, who came to be known as Peter de Erdington.

At the time of the Domesday survey in 1086, Erdington was still held by Peter and rated at three hides. It had arable land for six ploughs, a mill rated at three shillings and five acres of meadow and woods, one mile in length and half a mile in breadth. It was valued at thirty shillings. Peter's tenure would probably have been by 'knight's fee', which would have entailed his rendering military service to the Norman overlord for 40 days a year — an obligation which, in some cases, could be commuted to a payment of money in lieu of service.

Wilmot House, Sutton Road, Erdington

Despite Erdington's links with Aston, Yentonians would probably have been much more aware of those with Sutton Coldfield. Erdington lay within the bounds of Sutton Forest, and feudal tenants within its confines were subject to the harsh Norman forest laws, which forbade the hunting of wild animals and the keeping of sheep because, it was believed, their presence was detrimental to the royal deer, the feeding habits of which were similar to those of sheep.

But there were some rights, too, intended to offset to some extent the restrictions necessary to protect the royal game. Tenants had an allowance of timber from the forest for repairing tenements, known as 'house-bote', and a separate allowance of wood for the repair of fences, called 'hay-bote'. They also had free pasturage for their cattle.

Erdington remained within the precincts of the Royal Forest until 1126, when Henry I exchanged the Manor of Sutton, with its forest, for two manors in Rutland, belonging to Roger, Earl of Warwick. The forest thus became a chase, (it was only termed a forest when it belonged to the king).

Pype Manor House

Pype Hayes Hall

This brought some relaxation of the forest laws and the commencement of Sutton's long allegiance to the Earls of Warwick, broken only by the death of Warwick, termed 'the Kingmaker', at the Battle of Barnet in 1471.

Erdington's mill, referred to in Domesday, was at Bromford, a name suggesting 'the ford by which the broom flourishes'. It stood quite close to the manor-house on a loop of the river, across which a straight channel — known as a 'fleam' — was cut to facilitate the milling of corn. This mill belonged to the lord of the manor, and tenants were obliged to grind their corn there. The villagers' route to Bromford was down the winding Bromford Lane, described in earlier times as a narrow, mysterious lane between high banks, with trees meeting overhead. 'The Lad in the Lane' or 'Green Man' was probably built in the 14th century as a freeholder's house and was later converted into a village ale-house. Here, it may be surmised, the strong ale so bemused its patrons that Bromford Lane, in the course of the centuries and probably on the slenderest evidence, acquired a reputation for being haunted. 'The Lad in the Lane', in addition to being Erdington's oldest building, has been claimed to be the oldest inn in Warwickshire.* It

* Erdington, like Sutton Coldfield, was a part of Warwickshire until local government reorganisation in 1974.

14

was largely rebuilt in 1930, but part of its timber-framing, dating from the early 14th century, still survives. Standing, as it does, well back from the lane, it is thought that it may once have had its own gatehouse and court. This belief is based on the known fact that another medieval house, Benbow Place, later known as Wilmot House, (now demolished), which stood in Sutton Road, almost opposite Orchard Road, had a two-bay timber gatehouse in the 15th century.

The last thatched roof in Erdington: cottage in Fern Road
(E.H. Sargeant)

Old cottage in Moor End Lane

(Benjamin Stone)

Old cottage, Sutton Road

CHAPTER II

Plague and Civil War

W<small>E KNOW A LITTLE ABOUT</small> the early lords of the manor, one of whom — Thomas de Erdington, (a predecessor of the one referred to in Chapter I) — a man said to be of unscrupulous cunning, was appointed Chamberlain by King John. Dugdale tells us he 'received many great favours' from the king, but, in his later years, became a monk at Worcester. His eldest son, Peter, went crusading to the Holy Land, where he was slain, with the result that his younger brother, Giles, inherited the estate while he was still a minor.

Dugdale relates that in the reign of John there was a chapel within the precincts of Erdington manor-house, but because Erdington was a part of Aston, it had no church of its own. We do not know when the manor-house chapel fell into decay, but we know that it did because Dugdale, in describing the site, refers to 'an ancient chapel peculiar to the house, as by its ruins may be seen.'

The medieval tenants probably never saw the inside of the chapel within the lord's manor-house, neither did they build for themselves a 'chapel of ease', as was often done in remote hamlets. It is clear, too that they did not relish a long walk every Sunday, to and from church after a hard week's toil, for their attendance was lax. It is hardly surprising that, in an Age of Faith, the parish priest should have made known his displeasure at such a state of affairs. This resulted in Henry de Erdington making a conciliatory gesture towards the Mother Church of Aston in the fourteenth century. He added a south aisle to the church, which came to be known as the Erdington chantry, upon which he also bestowed an annual rent of sixpence to maintain the guttering.

Six hundred years ago the terrible 'Black Death' swept westwards across Europe from India. It reached England in 1349. The population of the country at the time was not quite four million, and the mortality rate was such that the sheep and cattle strayed through the corn and there was no-one to tend them. They, too, died, and their rotting bodies poisoned the air.

Old cottages Station Road, 1901

Erdington at that time was still a tiny place, although its population had grown since the time of the Domesday survey. Local 14th century records indicate that the hamlet suffered a setback, to be inferred from the fact that land in Erdington, which had only recently been brought into cultivation, reverted to waste after the Black Death had taken its toll. The local consequences of the plague in terms of human suffering can be measured from the case of Henry de Pipe, who owned the Manor of Pipe, (or Pype), within the precincts of Erdington. By his first wife, Ingrith, he had many children but, it is related, they all, except one girl child, died with their mother of the pestilence.

More trouble was to follow for Henry de Pipe when he took a second wife, Maud — daughter of George de Castello of Castle Bromwich. Dugdale tells us that, not long after the marriage, he found she was with child by a man named John Boote, his father's servant. This discovery seems to have been 'the last straw' for poor Henry, who died before the child was born, and his death, Dugdale relates, took place 'on the feast day of St. Laurence in the 36th year of the reign of Edward III.'

There seem to be few precise details relating to the extent of this Manor of Pipe — a manor within a manor. A house known as Pipe Manor-house, later Wood End House, was situated near the junction of Kingsbury Road and Wood End Road. To the east of Erdington and adjoining the Chester Road were what was known in the sixteenth century as 'The Pipe lands', acquired in that century by the Ardens of Park Hall in nearby Castle Bromwich, and added to their already extensive estate. The Ardens were one of the oldest families in England, whose destiny has been linked with that of Warwickshire for a thousand years. William Shakespeare himself was an Arden on his mother's side, and was said to be very proud of the fact. The name 'Pipe is derived from that of a small stream, a tributary of the River Tame, which, before discharging into that river, fed the double moat of Erdington's own manor-house.

In the reign of Elizabeth I., Edward Arden of Park Hall, Sheriff of Warwickshire in 1575, became involved in a plot against the Queen, which resulted in his being beheaded at Smithfield in 1583. As a consequence the Park Hall estate was for a while forfeited to the Crown before being

Old cottage behind Wood End House
(William A. Clark, F.R.P.S.)

19

eventually recovered by the Arden family. It was only a short while before the conviction of Edward Arden that the 'Pipe lands' had come into his family's possession, and at the time of his death, enclosure of the estate had not been completed. Nevertheless, a Court Roll for 1583 makes reference to 'a parcel of enclosed land, commonly called 'Pypehaye'', a 'haye' signifying a place surrounded by a hedge, often an enclosure made for the purposes of the chase. The same connotation is found in the French 'haie', a hedge; the German verb 'hagen' to hedge and the English 'hawthorn', originally hedge-thorn.

The Pype Hayes estate passed to Hervey Bagot when he married Dorothy, daughter of Sir Henry Arden of Park Hall early in the 17th century. Pype Hayes Hall was built by Bagot following his marriage — a task which took 12 years to complete. The second son of Hervey Bagot was a casualty of the Civil War. He was a Colonel in the Royalist forces and a one-time military governor of Lichfield, who was killed at the Battle of Naseby in 1645.

The Jacobean Pype Hayes Hall, sometimes called 'the house of the 13 gables', has been considerably altered over the centuries. It continued to be

Old cottages—Chester Road, near Sutton Road junction, October 1938

the home of successive generations of Bagots, one of whom — the Rev. Walter Bagot — was a friend of William Cowper, the poet. When Robert Southey, writer, poet-laureate and author of 'The Life of Nelson', was writing a biography of Cowper, he stayed at Pype Hayes Hall to copy letters written by the poet to Walter Bagot. In 1919, the Hall was acquired by Birmingham Corporation, when it was turned into a convalescent home, and the grounds then became a public park. After the Second World War the Hall was converted into a children's residential nursery.

Near Pype Hayes Hall stood a lodge, known as 'Bow Bearer's Lodge' where, in medieval times, two bowmen — retainers of the Earl of Warwick — were stationed. Their job was to conduct travellers along the Chester Road and across the wilds of Sutton Coldfield Chase, a region which for centuries had a reputation for being the haunt of vagabonds and robbers. The lodge, which has been described as a very old, strongly built cottage, was demolished in 1828, but early in this century there was still a field at Pype Hayes, known as 'Bow Bearer's Croft', the location of which is commemorated in the name of 'Bowcroft Grove'.

Prior to the passing of the various local enclosure acts of the 18th and early 19th centuries, much common land survived in the district. Near the junction of Chester Road and Bell Lane, Hollyfast Common was, in John Wesley's day, said to be a place where Methodist preachers came from Birmingham to hold open-air services. There is a graphic description of such a meeting in Chapter II of George Eliot's *Adam Bede.'*

After some legal wrangling in the late 14th century, the Manor of Aston came into the possession of the Holte family. In 1460 John Holte was made Ranger of Sutton Chase by Henry VI, and because he was a great favourite of that monarch, Dugdale referred to him contemptuously as a 'menial servant'. During the reign of Henry VIII, Thomas Holte, a Bencher of the Middle Temple and Lord of Aston, held several official posts and was described as 'a learned lawyer'. It was not, however, until 1571 that, with the birth of another Thomas Holte, the family entered upon its most prosperous era. After having been appointed Sheriff for the county in 1599, Thomas Holte became a member of the county deputation set up to welcome James VI of Scotland to the throne of England in April, 1603. James Stuart, who became James I of England, took a month to travel from Edinburgh to London, and he was met at each county boundary by the local gentry and escorted by them across the breadth of the shire. For the part he played in this ritual, Thomas Holte was knighted, and a few years later was created a baronet.

Chester Road, Sutton Road junction

Sir Thomas Holte's fortunes were further improved by 'a good marriage' and the family home at Duddeston soon ceased to be adequate for his needs. In April, 1618, after having enclosed a park at Aston, he started to build Aston Hall — a task which was to engross his time and resources for the next 17 years. When the civil war broke out in 1642, Holte was an old man, but although unfit for military service, he came down clearly on the Royalist side and gave financial help to King Charles I. By this time he was well established in Aston Hall where, it is said: 'he resided in great splendour, his ample resources enabling him to maintain in due state the dignity of his rank.'

In October, 1642, King Charles, whose army was marching from Shrewsbury to the relief of Banbury Castle, stayed two nights at the Hall. The following year, when it was garrisoned with Royalist troops, it was besieged by the Parliamentarians, and the mark of the cannon can still be seen on the main staircase. The Royalists surrendered after two days of combat, and the Hall was plundered. Sir Thomas was, for a time, imprisoned, and his financial loss as a result of the war was said to be £20,000.

Sutton Road, near the junction of Chester Road, (looking south)

The local family which had taken the name of Erdington for its own was extinguished in 1468, and thereafter the manor changed hands a number of times. It was for a short while in the possession of the Duke of Clarence, brother of Edward IV and Richard III before being acquired by Sir Thomas Holte in 1647. Many of the landlords of the interregnum were absentee ones, but the Dymocks, who came from south-east Warwickshire, resided at Erdington Hall between 1550 and 1615, and we have reason to believe that they were very unpopular with their tenants. This was probably because they were 'felden' landlords, who brought harsh and alien manorial laws from the south to the north of the county. The 'felden' was the open Warwickshire countryside to the south of the River Avon as opposed to the 'woodland' lying to the north of the river which, by tradition, was always more heavily forested than the rest of the county.

The Dymocks' strictness over tenants' obligations led to much opposition at Erdington, particularly, it seems, over the payment of heriot where, on the death of a tenant, the heir had to forfeit the deceased's best beast or chattel to the lord of the manor. When Sir Henry Dymock — the last of the 'felden' landlords — died in 1615, it is recorded in the Aston Church register that:

Entrance to the Dwarf Holes

(Benjamin Stone)

"Sir Henry Dymock of Erdington, Knight, was burried ye fifte day of Octr. at one of ye clocke in ye morninge, for whom nothing was done at all, not so much as a bell rung."

Dymock was a bachelor, which may have accounted for the lack of family mourners at his funeral, and it is hardly surprising that his stubborn and resentful tenants should not have turned out for the occasion.

The resistance to authority on the part of the Erdington tenants was rather more passive than active and, tempered with a good measure of rustic guile, it enabled them to avoid any deep involvement in outside affairs. At the time of the civil war the villagers, with a rising population, were probably too busy extending their agricultural encroachments into the surrounding common land to have much time to think about the pros and cons of the Royalist and Parliamentarian causes. In 1643, because Birmingham was largely a centre of Parliamentary support and had refused to supply arms to the king's men, Prince Rupert, nephew of Charles I., came to punish the town. The Birmingham defenders, who were heavily outnumbered, suffered a crushing defeat, there was killing and looting and some 80 houses and other buildings were burnt to the ground.

After his Birmingham victory, Prince Rupert, with his troops, passed through Erdington and Sutton Coldfield on their way to Lichfield. But whatever their views may have been — and it is known that there was considerable anti-Royalist feeling in the district — it is unlikely that the Erdington villagers would, by word, deed or gesture, have revealed their sympathies.

Sir Thomas Holte

Bell Lane (later Orphanage Road), near the Village Green

Old cottages, butcher's shop and garage in Sutton Road, opposite the Abbey

CHAPTER III

The Changing Scene

CHESTER ROAD is probably the oldest local road, while Bromford Lane and the Birmingham — Lichfield portway* are both of some antiquity. The importance of the Chester Road is due, in part, to it being the route taken by the Welsh drovers when they brought their herds to the markets of the Midlands and the south-east. Almost everyone in Erdington eked out a precarious living from the land and the numerous scattered farms and smallholdings of the impoverished tenants were linked by rough paths or tracks, known as 'fordroughs'. In the course of time these tracks developed into many of the roads we know today. These include Wood End Lane, Short Heath Road, Summer Road, Moor End Lane, Orphanage Road, Holly Lane, Church Road, Spring Lane, Marsh Hill and Court Lane. The High Street appears to have been in existence since at least the 14th century. Reservoir Road was once known as Luckock's Lane, named after a local farmer and — less reputably — as 'Cut-throat Lane', while Slade Road suggests a path through a valley, 'slade' being Old English for valley.

The direct route to Birmingham by way of Salford Bridge led down Gravelly Hill, described by John Leland in the 16th century as being 'by sandy ground, better wooded than fertile of wheat . . . the soil is sandy and dry and good for conyes', (rabbits). Gravelly Hill long remained as a rabbit warren and a place considered to be unworthy of cultivation. Not surprisingly, links between Erdington and fast-growing Birmingham long remained of a tenuous nature.

At the bottom of Gravelly Hill, spanning the River Tame, was Salford Bridge, which was originally only a footbridge, with a ford for carts and other vehicles. It was not until 1810 that a bridge suitable for traffic was built across the river at this point. Salford Bridge was mentioned in a document of Henry III's reign, in which it appeared as 'Shrafford Brugge'.

---

* Portway: a path leading to a market town.

*Station Road, Erdington was known as Sheep Lane before the coming of the railway
Some old property can still be seen there*

*The old dairy, formerly a farm-house, a late Georgian building in Station Road,
now demolished*

Shrafford is a word of Saxon origin, signifying 'the ford by the caves'. The caves were natural, water-formed cavities in the face of the nearby Copeley Hill escarpment, which led to several artificially enlarged caverns of considerable size. They survived until the 1939-1945 war, during which they were converted into air-raid shelters, in which form they remained until they were finally obliterated by the construction of the huge multi-level motorway interchange, known unofficially to most local people as 'Spaghetti Junction'.

The Salford Bridge caves have been called the oldest work of man in the district. In a deed of 1490 they were referred to as 'the Dwarf Holes', and nearby there was a Dwarf Hole Mill and a Dwarf Hole Meadow. But who those diminutive cave-dwellers might have been is left very much to the imagination. One thing, however, is certain: if anyone ever managed to live in those damp and porous sandstone caverns above the River Tame at Salford Bridge, they must have been especially hardy — and possibly a little rheumaticky, too.

In a small volume of verse entitled *Rhymes, Grave, Gay, and Otherwise*, the locality is commemorated in a long poem, called 'Copeley Hill', written in 1876 by Thomas Townsend. Despite his disclaimer over prophecy, the lines:

> My Muse claims no Vision of Prophecy, still
> Let me dream of thy future, fair Copeley Hill!
> Will some levelling Brummagem Mayor of the day
> In some vast Improvement Scheme sweep thee away . . .

might be considered by some to contain a hint of the shape of things to come with the making of 'Spaghetti Junction' almost a century later.

William Hutton, writing in the 18th century of the roads out of Birmingham, tells us: 'Many of them were worn by the practice of ages into hollow-ways, 12 or 14 yards below the banks with which they were once even'.* They were extremely narrow, since wheeled vehicles were so little used. The commencement of the coaching era in that century led, eventually, to considerable improvement, brought about by the turnpiking of roads and the paying of tolls by those people who travelled upon them.

A Turnpike Act was passed in 1759 in respect of the Chester Road, but it was not until 1807 that a similar act was passed covering the road from Birmingham, through Erdington Village. Subsequently the High Street rang

---

* The name of 'Holloway Head' in Birmingham reminds us of one such old road.

29

Terry's Lane (Eachelhurst Road)

to the sound of the stage coaches, plying on the long haul between Bristol and the North of England, a fact which, no doubt, contributed to some slight lessening of Erdington's age-old insularity.

Chester Road was on the stage coach route between London and Chester — then the port of embarkation for Ireland. That road was wild, lonely and ill-kept, with a long reputation for being the haunt of highway robbers. The coaches travelled from dawn to dusk with stops for passengers to sleep at inns en route and the journey took six days.

In 1784 the first stage-coaches to carry mail as well as passengers went into service. They had armed guards as protection against robbers and were exempt from turnpike tolls. They had a reputation for high speeds and following the improvements to the road the 'Irish Mail' was able to traverse the Chester Road at some speed and with little interference from the numerous highwaymen in the district.

Erdington in the mid-18th century had a population of just under 700. Within its boundaries there were 52 roads and lanes, one forge, 40 farms, 96 cottages, two smithies and a shop. Among the early hostelries were the 'Bull's Head' and the 'White Lion' in the High Street, the 'Swan' by the Village Green and the 'Cross Keys' on the corner of Sheep Lane, (now Station Road). At Chester Road stood the 'Bell and Cuckoo', which assumed considerable importance during the coaching era, standing as it did at the crossing of two turnpike roads, and in Bromford Lane the 'Green Man' was already old.

Birmingham during the same period was growing fast. Both its trade and population were increasing, and it needed to have a cheap and ready means of bringing in raw material for its growing industries and of conveying its products to distant markets. The result over a relatively short period of time was the construction of a network of canals which was to revolutionise transportation in a way no less drastic than that which was to follow the coming of the railways some 75 years later.

The Birmingham — Fazeley Canal, when completed in 1783, lay along Erdington's southern boundary, and was described as being ' . . . across the River Tame below Salford Bridge in the said Parish of Aston-juxta-Birmingham and by the side of a messuage belonging to the said Heneage

Farm in Bell Lane

(Benjamin Stone)

31

The scene of a murder, (see page 33) Penns Lane in 1817, drawn and etched by Samuel Lines, a famous local artist

Legge* called Erdington Hall . . .' It was specified that 'the canal or any works appertaining thereto should not be built within 500 yards of Pipe Hall, belonging to the Rev. Walter Bagot, Clerk.' In the planning stage of canals, land-owners were frequently able to make stipulations or modifications of various kinds to protect their own estates. Sir Henry Gough of Edgbaston Hall, for instance, insisted that the canal towpath near his estate should be on the opposite side of the canal to that of the hall.

The canal era brought cheap coal to Birmingham homes from the Black Country, but it is doubtful whether, in the short term, the Birmingham — Fazeley Canal did anything to improve the lot of Yentonians. In later times, however, it brought some prosperity to the area, due to industrialists being induced to build factories along the canal banks by the offer of low cost coal and the statutory right to use canal water for their static steam-engines.

*   *   *   *   *

---

* Heneage Legge inherited the Manor on the extinction of the Holte baronetcy in 1782.

On the morning of Tuesday, 27th May, 1817, the body of a young woman was found, drowned in a marl-pit in Penns Lane. The victim was Mary Ashford, aged 20, whose home was in High Street, Erdington. The previous day — Whit Monday — she had spent the evening at a dance at Tyburn House, where she had danced almost exclusively with a man named Abraham Thornton from Castle Bromwich. There were witnesses who said that the two had also been seen together after the dance.

Thornton was arrested and charged with murder, but due to the inconclusive nature of the evidence he was acquitted. Mary Ashford's brother, William, then took out a private summons against Thornton, and a fresh trial ensued. As it was an appeal against an earlier decision, more than one judge heard the case, which was presided over by the Lord Chief Justice, Lord Ellenborough. The defendant, when asked in court whether or not he was guilty, replied in a loud, clear voice: 'Not Guilty, and I am ready to defend the same with my body!' whereupon he threw a gauntlet to the floor of the court, at the same time challenging William Ashford to a duel. This

Salford Bridge, junction of Tyburn Road and Gravelly Hill — 1925

Salford Bridge—Gravelly Hill junction, before and after alterations and rebuilding of bridge in 1926

Marsh Hill, 1923

was known as invoking 'wager by battle', an almost forgotten legal right which had not been exercised for centuries.

Ashford was no match for the burly Thornton, and the challenge was not taken up, which meant that the accused man was released. Within the shortest possible time, however, 'wager by battle' was abolished by parliament, and the case became part of English legal history, known to law students as 'Ashford v. Thornton'. Mary Ashford's grave can be seen in the churchyard of Holy Trinity Church, Sutton Coldfield.

Rural outlook from Copeley Hill

Parish Church, Erdington.

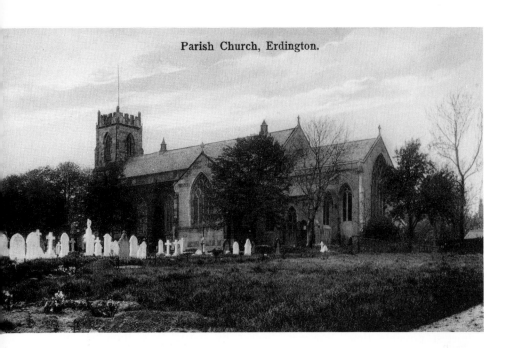

Sutton Road, viewed from the High Street

CHAPTER IV

Churches, Law Enforcement and Transport

IN 1824, WITH A POPULATION OF UNDER 2,000, Erdington acquired a church of its own, and in the same year the National School in the High Street was completed. Because at that time Erdington was still a part of Aston, as it remained until 1894, the church was first known as the St. Barnabas Chapel-of-Ease, but in 1858 Erdington became a separate ecclesiastical district with its own vicar. The first stone of the building was laid by Earl Howe on 17th June, 1822, he having donated the land upon which the church was to be built. Work on a Roman Catholic Church, later to become known as the Abbey, was started in 1848 and completed two years later. Other churches and schools were built during the century.

At the 1851 census the population of Erdington had risen to 2,579 — a population which included 17 farmers and 9 publicans. There were, by then, 442 houses in the Village, but surrounding areas remained sparsely populated. Between Erdington and Witton, for instance, there were, in the mid-19th century, only a few scattered houses and cottages, seven of which were at Stockland Green.

Law and order were maintained by a solitary constable named John Pearson. There was a lock-up and magistrates' court in Bell Lane, (later Orphanage Road), from whence any offender committed to prison had to be conveyed by the constable to the county gaol at Warwick. Prize-fighting and cock-fighting, both of which were illegal, were popular in the district, and from time to time the constable was knocked about by ruffians who came to the Village to poach. There was said to be scarcely a house between the church and the Swan Inn, and the road was flanked by farm-land. The passer-by in the High Street, on looking over the hedge to the west would have had a distant view of Barr Beacon. Opposite the Village Green, on the

The Prince of Wales, later Edward VII, on the occasion of the opening of the Jaffray Hospital

site of the present library, stood the Erdington Workhouse, described as 'an old ramshackle building.'

An interesting memento of Erdington's rural past is in the possession of the Applied Arts Department of the Birmingham City Museum. It is a fine white linen smock, which belonged to Uriah Barlow of Erdington, (1789-1861), and it can be inspected by appointment, when not on display, quoting the reference M.54-62. Smocks were frequently worn by agricultural workers, but patterned ones such as this were usually kept for wearing on Sundays.

The Victorian virtue of self-help could not have been better exemplified than in Josiah Mason, a poor boy from Kidderminster who, without formal education, made great wealth in Birmingham from the trades of steel-pen making and electro-plating. He came to live at Erdington, and it was here that he conceived the idea of doing something to alleviate the poverty and suffering which he saw around him. In 1858 he built almshouses and a small orphanage at the junction of the High Street and Station Road. This, however, did not fully reflect the measure of his philanthropy, and in 1865 he embarked on what the local press was later to call 'one of the noblest works of charity in our time, or perhaps in any time'. The building of an orphanage, together with almshouses at the junction of Chester Road and

Workers at Nock's Brickworks, Erdington, 1890

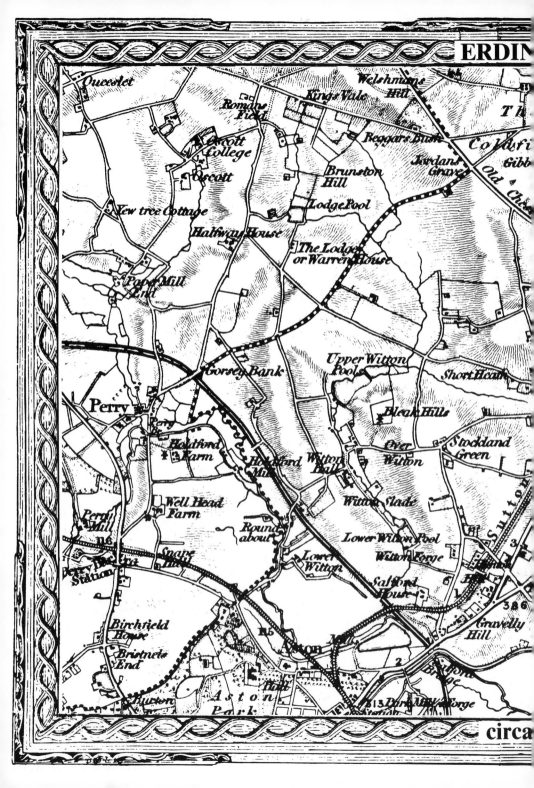

Ouesslet

Romans Field

King's Vale

Welshmuns Hill

Co Wasfi

Gibb

Beggars Bush

Jordans Graves

Old Ches

Cscott College

Cscott

Brunston Hill

Yew tree Cottage

Lodge Pool

Halfway House

The Lodge
or Warren House

Paper Mill End

Upper Witton Pools

Short Heath

Gorsey Bank

Perry

Bleak Hills

Perry

Over Witton

Stockland Green

Holdford Farm

Holdford Mill

Witton Hall

Well Head Farm

Witton Slade

Round about

Lower Witton Pool

Sutton

Perry Mill

Witton Forge

Snape Hill

Perry Barr Station

Lower Witton

Salford House

Birchfield House

Gravelly Hill

Bristnels End

Aston

Burton

Aston Park

Hall

Brdeton Bridge

Park Mill Forge

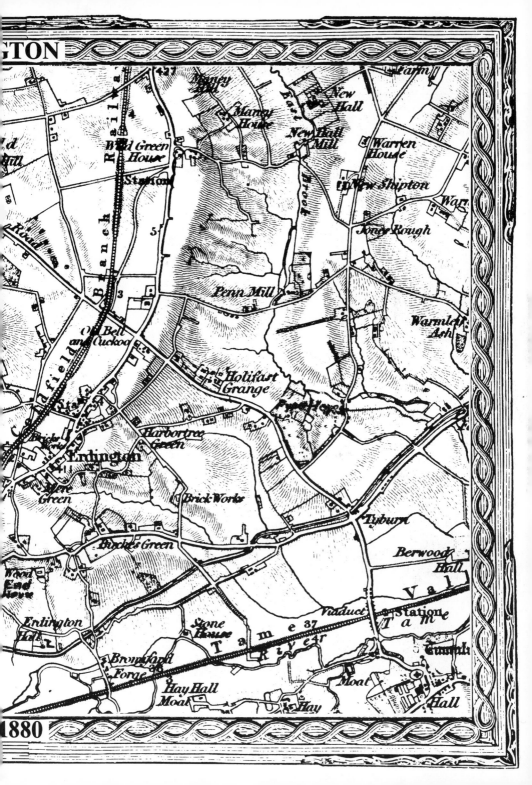

Canal Bridge, Bromford Lane

Sir Josiah Mason's Orphanage and Mausoleum

Bell Lane, (later Orphanage Road) proceeded with the minimum of publicity and, on completion, its 250 ft. tower became a landmark for miles around. It was formally opened in 1869 and survived until 1964, when it was demolished. In 1875 Josiah Mason laid the first stone of the College in Edmund Street, Birmingham which bore his name. It later formed the nucleus of Birmingham University, the main building of which was opened at Edgbaston by King Edward VII in 1909. Mason College was demolished in 1963.

Another local worthy of the same period was Benjamin Stone, who lived at the Grange, Erdington. Successful industrialist, member of parliament for East Birmingham from 1895 to 1909 and first mayor of Sutton Coldfield, Stone is remembered today for his supreme skill as a photographer and his gift to posterity of 26,000 photographs. Benjamin Stone was knighted in 1892 and the culmination of his photographic career came in 1911, when he was appointed official photographer at the Coronation of King George V.

When the London and North Western Railway extended its line between Birmingham and Aston to Sutton Coldfield in 1862, Erdington, though still a quiet village, earning its living by age-old agricultural pursuits, became 'ripe for suburban development'. By 1891, due largely to the coming of the

Sir Josiah Mason's Almshouses, Station Road

Boys' Classroom, Mason's Orphanage — 1908 (Benjamin Stone)

Girls' Classroom Mason's Orphanage — 1908 (Benjamin Stone)

railway, the population had shot up to 9,269. Erdington Station was in Sheep Lane, which later became known as Station Road, where there were only a few cottages and pools on either side of the road. There were other stations at Gravelly Hill and Chester Road.

Erdington's other link with Birmingham was provided by a horse 'bus service, plying between Sutton and New Street, Birmingham, which ran through the Village two or three times daily, with its loading point outside the Swan Inn. From 1885 the 'buses worked in conjunction with the Aston steam-trams, which had their outer terminus at Salford Bridge. The steam-trams, which were coke-fired, were dirty and smoky; they were also bad on hills and incapable of climbing Gravelly Hill.

The horse 'buses had a speed restriction of 5 m.p.h., and the operators were required to provide the inside of each 'bus with clean straw on the floor in cold weather. When it was foggy the horse had to wear a bell. There was seating for eight passengers inside and six on top and the driver collected fares through a trap-door.

At the turn of the century, despite a continuing rise in population, Erdington was still a sleepy place. It had no police-station; no fire-station;

Maid-servants at The Grange, (the home of Benjamin Stone), July 1899
(Benjamin Stone)

45

*Wedding at Erdington parish church of Dora Stone
and Dr. McKenzie, July, 1899*　　　　*(Benjamin Stone)*

*A proposal to build a gas works beside Kingsbury Road
at Birches Green was defeated due to strong local opposition*

Six Ways, early in the present century

no street-lamps; no library and no telephone service. Following upon formation of the Urban District Council in 1894 — which had its offices at 'The Rookery', Kingsbury Road, the grounds of which now form Rookery Park — the Village underwent many changes. New roads and footpaths were made; sewers were put in; houses built and street lighting installed.

In 1907, Erdington made two notable acquisitions — its first tramway, powered by electricity, and its free library. The library was not a controversial issue, as its building was financed entirely by Andrew Carnegie, the philanthropist. But the tramway, when first proposed, was a different matter. Its route to Chester Road meant that tramcars would traverse Gravelly Hill and Sutton Road — both thoroughfares along which stood large houses, the homes of prominent members of the local community. Opposition to the plan stiffened.

It was claimed that the tramcars would endanger the lives of people — particularly children _ when crossing the roads; frighten horses and, by causing residences to be overlooked from the trams, to reduce their value. It was also said that the rural aspect of the district would be ruined. 'Crush the monster!' was the rallying cry to ratepayers.

One man who did much to overcome local opposition to the tramcar was William Lee who, in addition to being Chairman of the Tramways

Erdington tram terminus in 1913 — the year in which a 'bus service first provided a link between this, the Erdington boundary, and Sutton Parade

Committee in Birmingham was also a member of Erdington UDC. His moment of triumph came in the spring of 1907, when he drove the first tramcar to the Sutton boundary at Harman Road. Other routes were opened later — to Stockland Green in 1912, extended to Short Heath in 1926 and to Holly Lane by sleeper-track along the then new Tyburn Road in 1920, extended to Pype Hayes in 1927. In 1938 the Erdington trams were diverted from the High Street along Sutton New Road on its completion.

The making of the tram-track along Tyburn Road was designed to serve the needs of workers at the Dunlop Rubber Company's factory at Fort Dunlop, the company having moved there from their premises at Aston Cross in 1916. On account of the inaccessibility of the new factory to its workers, the management provided them with water transport along the canal. In 1919 there were said to be five converted narrow-boats, each seating 100 workers, doing half-hour journeys between Aston and Fort Dunlop, mornings and evenings. Because of the watery approach to their work-place, employees referred to it as 'Port Dunlop', but the subsequent official name, 'Fort Dunlop' may be accounted for by the fact that 'dun' is Gaelic for 'fort'.

The cutting of the new road, known originally as Salford Bridge Road, through the lower slopes of Gravelly Hill involved excavating through a considerable amount of hard red sandstone, and the work had to be abandoned for several years due to the Great War. The laying of the tram-track to Holly Lane was no easy matter. It involved an enormous amount of excavating for the making of the track reservation and the laying down of over 10,000 tons of ballast, as well as 7,800 sleepers. The whole of the work was accomplished by the Tramways Department in four months, and that included 30 wet days.

The several new tram routes served housing developments in what had been farm land on Erdington's perimeter. These included estates at Birches Green; Pype Hayes; Court Farm and Stockland Green. The trams continued to serve local needs until 1953, by which time Birmingham's former fleet of 843 trams had dwindled to those operating on three routes — Erdington, Short Heath and Pype Hayes. On Saturday, 4th July of that year, Yentonians, who had once so reviled 'the monster', turned out in crowds to wave flags and cheer the last tram on its way to the scrapyard. The switch-over to 'buses took place without any loss of continuity of service.

A memento of the year 1897

49

The Village Green, decorated for the Coronation of Edward VII, 1902

FRIDAY, JUNE 27,
THE AGED POOR OF 50 YEARS AND UPWARDS
Will be provided with
A DINNER
In a MARQUEE erected in Mr. Councillor WILTON'S Field, WILTON ROAD, at 2 o'clock p.m.
ENTERTAINMENTS WILL BE GIVEN AFTER THE DINNER.

ADMISSION BY TICKET ONLY.

"GOD SAVE THE KING."
A. H. SAXTON, Printer, Six Ways, Erdington.

Old age came early in 1902!

CHAPTER V

The 20th Century's Impact on 'The Village'

AT THE BEGINNING of the 20th century there was probably little evidence of the vast changes which were soon to transform Erdington from the role of an agricultural village to that of the thriving and largely industrialised suburb we know today. In 1894, having achieved the status of an Urban District Council, it obtained independence from Aston. But there were already indications of future changes. Erdington under its UDC. depended on Birmingham for its gas, water supply and, after 1907, its tramway system, and some of its more percipient inhabitants may not have been wholly surprised when the Village was absorbed by Birmingham in 1911. At the same time Aston Manor, Handsworth, Yardley and Kings Norton were brought within the city boundaries, creating a 'Greater Birmingham' increased three-fold in size.

We have a glimpse of Erdington High Street in 1911 from the pen of a newspaper correspondent, signing himself 'an old Yentonian':

"The straight stretch of main road between the Six Ways and the Church has been converted into a fine boulevard, affording a wide roadway, with ample room for the tram-lines, and having unusually deep pavements. The result of this has been the shifting of the business hub of Erdington some hundreds of yards nearer Birmingham."

The motor car was a rarity in those days and horse traffic predominated on the roads, many of them unmacadamised. Mr C. J. R. Yates of Sutton Coldfield recalls that as late as c.1922 an old man used to sit at the roadside in Court Lane, opposite the 'Greyhound', whose job it was to break up stones with a long handled hammer to make flints for the roads. The stones were brought to him in carts drawn by four horses. There were still country walks around Erdington and enough wayside wild flowers for children to

Tom Green, Erdington's first appointed postman, who was burned to death in 1928 at the age of 81

Erdington Free Library, opening ceremony, July 2, 1907

Snow scene, February, 1912

make garlands. At the end of Wood End Lane there was a pool on which people used to skate in winter.

The moving picture era — the age of the cinema — was heralded in Erdington before the Great War by the opening of three cinemas. In 1912 the public hall in the High Street was converted into the 'Palace'; the following year the cosy little 'Picture House', also in the High Street, opened its doors for the first time and in April, 1914 the 'Star Cinema' in Slade Road was completed. In the inter-war years, with an ever-increasing enthusiasm for 'going to the pictures', two more cinemas were built in the district — the 'Plaza' at Stockland Green in 1927 and the 'Pavilion' at Chester Road, Wylde Green in 1931. One real-life rags to riches story worthy of a film scenario was enacted when a young girl named Violet Pretty, an usherette at the 'Palace', later became a film star, re-named Anne Heywood. None of the cinemas has survived.

One event more than any other which contributed to the ending of Erdington's long centuries of non-involvement in outside affairs was the Great War of 1914-1918. Following upon Britain's declaration of war on

Germany on 4th August, 1914, a fervour of patriotism swept the country. There was an unprecedented rush to the colours, prompted in part by the popular belief that the war would be over by Christmas and that, without haste in joining up, the thrill of having participated in so stirring an event would be missed.

Erdington's 'flea pit', built in 1913

Erdington Roller Skating Rink, Orphanage Road

1915

*A sad aftermath of the Great War
of 1914-1918*

Posters urging young men to 'Join the Army today — Your King and Country need you!' appeared on every hoarding and recruiting meetings were held up and down the country. One such mass meeting took place in the Palace Cinema on 7th September, 1914, the purpose of which was, according to the poster 'to explain the Country's need and to support Lord Kitchener's patriotic appeal'. Admission, it was added, was free, with a footnote: 'Ladies admitted to balcony only'.

The youth of Erdington was not slow to respond and many young men joined one or other of the 'City Battalions' of the Royal Warwickshire Regiment. For those who didn't enlist in 1914, further pressure was brought to bear upon them, urging them to do so, and in 1916 military service became obligatory.

The war continued for over four years and its horrors were reflected in the long casualty lists. Erdington, like every other town and village in the country, paid a heavy price in human suffering. At a memorial service in Erdington Parish Church in 1919, the names of 109 men of the parish were recorded on a nominal roll of those 'killed in action, or who have died of wounds or disease during the Great European War'.

Gravelly Lane, June 1926

Birth of a tramway — before, during and after

The work on Slade Road extension, which became Streetly Road.
In 1926 the tram route was extended from Stockland Green to Short Heath.

High Street, Erdington, 1929

During the two decades following the Great War, Erdington continued to grow, with new estates springing up on its perimeter and increased industrialisation in the Tyburn Road — Kingsbury Road — Chester Road areas, facilitated by good rail, road and canal cummunications. Erdington's central and strategically important position in the country was emphasised in 1920 when, in nearby Castle Bromwich, the British Industries Fair held its first exhibition of Birmingham's industrial products — an event which was subsequently held annually in a vast, purpose-built exhibition hall.

In 1925 Erdington acquired its own swimming baths in Mason Road on what had been, in earlier times, the workhouse field. In the following year the 'Outer Circle' 'bus route was inaugurated. This service, encircling Birmingham's outer suburbs, passed through Erdington at Six Ways, so linking the Village with many other parts of the city. Improved educational facilities were provided to cater for Erdington's growing population, and in 1931 an open-air school was built at Marsh Hill to accommodate what were described officially as 'weakly, debilitated and anaemic children'.

Erdington, too, had a place in the 'racing calendar'. Birmingham Racecourse at Bromford Bridge was a popular venue in the inter-war years, and special 'buses for punters ran from the city to the races. The last race meeting was in 1965 and the site is now occupied by the Bromford Bridge estate.

In 1938 Sutton New Road was completed, work on which had entailed a considerable amount of demolition of old property. When it was opened, much through traffic was diverted from Erdington High Street, including the trams, which, prior to the making of the new road, had to operate on single track through the narrow part of the High Street.

War with Germany broke out again in 1939. Erdington had the unenviable distinction of being the first Birmingham suburb to be bombed. On 9th August, 1940, eight bombs were dropped by a solitary German raider over a wide area of Erdington, resulting in casualties and damage to property — and the city's first fatality through enemy action. The victim was a young soldier, home on leave from his unit. It is highly probable that the pilot had intended to bomb either Fort Dunlop or the Bromford Tubular Rolling Mills, for it is known that the Germans had planned their destruction several months before the war started. At Castle Bromwich over 12,000 'planes were built during the war in what became the biggest aircraft factory in Europe. This was one of the 'shadow factories', so called on account of the secrecy involved. This however did not prevent numerous

Six Ways, before and after the making of Sutton New Road

air-raids on the premises, with some casualties. Peace was restored in 1945 after a war vastly different in its nature from its predecessor, with many casualties among the civilian population and less among those in the armed forces than in the 1914-1918 conflict.

The post-war era has been marked locally, as in so many other places, by the sweeping away of many old and familiar landmarks in and around the Village and much rebuilding. Shops, pubs, houses, cinemas, churches and the National School in the High Street have disappeared and, in many cases, they have been replaced by buildings totally lacking in character. The demolition of the fine Victorian houses along the western side of Sutton Road, Erdington was probably inevitable. They were designed to function with servants, so necessary to upper middle class society in the 19th century, and, other than by converting them into flats, they were too big for modern requirements. But Wilmot House (see page 12) was a different matter. Its destruction in the late 'fifties was an act of official vandalism of the first magnitude. The Sutton Road site was cleared to make way for the Lyndhurst Estate, the high-rise nature of which dominates the skyline. Harlech Tower, built in 1960, was the first 16-storey block of flats in the city. The estate's redeeming feature is the large number of mature trees and shrubs which have been retained.

It would be impossible to write even a short history of Erdington in the late 20th century without reference to that monstrous monument to the motor-car, 'Spaghetti Junction', on Erdington's southern boundary. The Gravelly Hill Interchange — to give it its proper name — was commenced in 1967 as part of a huge motorway link-up. Work upon it entailed diverting the course of the River Tame, demolishing homes and rehousing families, while noise and lead pollution have continued to blight lives and properties still in the vicinity.

In 1971 the 'Green Man' in Bromford Lane — Erdington's oldest building — was given what was described as a 'face-lift'. Fortunately, however, neither this nor the previous work carried out in 1930 has deprived the inn of its aura of antiquity, engendered by its surviving ancient timber-framing. Following refurbishing, the 'Green Man' reverted to its former name, 'The Lad in the Lane', a name said to have associations with spring fertility rites, as described by Sir James Frazer, the folk-lorist and author of 'The Golden Bough'.

Fears were expressed during the 'seventies over the decline of Erdington High Street as a popular shopping area, attributed in part to the dearth of parking sites. The decline was high-lighted when Owen Owen's store ceased

Sutton New Road in the making, February 1938

Harman Road extension, later Berwood Farm Road, 1938
(E.H. Sargeant)

trading, leaving the building a large, empty shell. During the same period, Erdington Market also experienced a drop in customers and the opinion was voiced that Erdington was being neglected, while Sutton Coldfield's shopping facilities were being lavishly expanded.

Public disquiet and considerable protest were caused by the opening of the top-security Glenthorne Youth Treatment Centre at Kingsbury Road in 1978, which was to house young people with 'serious behavioural problems'. It was pointed out, however, that not all the occupants would be people with criminal records.

In late 1983 an interesting bit of 'industrial archaeology' came to light when road work in the High Street prior to pedestrianisation revealed a section of tram-track, which had been covered over following the diversion of the trams from the High Street to Sutton New Road in 1938. Pedestrianisation of the High Street between Mason Road and New Street was completed in 1984 at a cost of £65,000, funded by the West Midlands County Council. Not everyone, however, was happy about the change, as small traders claimed that it would hit their businesses.

Several ward boundary changes have taken place over the years, making it difficult to assess Erdington's population trends in recent times. Figures from the 1981 Census, however, provide some revealing facts. Erdington's population in 1981 was 35,289, compared with 39,708 in 1971, but this has to be seen in the light of boundary changes which took place under local government reorganisation in 1974. The sexes were almost evenly balanced, with 17,247 males and 18,042 females. The total immigrant population of Erdington was not shown in the statistics, but there were two categories listed, those 'Born outside the United Kingdom, 7.5%' and 'Households with head born in New Commonwealth or Pakistan, 3.8%': Out of a total of 13,248 Erdington households, 43.5% were in owner-occupation and 48.1% of householders were car-owners.

In an age of great mobility and floating populations, the number of inhabitants with deep roots in 'the Village', whose families have lived here for generations, was not revealed in the statistics.

Preparing for pedestrianisation — 1984
(Birmingham Post and Mail)

CHAPTER VI

Near Neighbours

W ITTON, TO THE UNINITIATED, is a dull, industrialised place, notorious as a 'bottleneck' for traffic plying between Sutton Coldfield and Birmingham. Yet is has a history distinct from that of either Erdington or Aston, its near neighbours. Before the Conquest, the freehold of this small manor belonged to Staunchel, a Saxon landowner, and like so many other places in the district, it came into the possession of that powerful Norman overlord, William Fitz-Ausculf. But, as Dugdale tells us:

> ' . . . the same Staunchel became tenant to this new lord (as generally the native English were constrain'd to do); so that at the time of the Conqueror's Survey it was certified, with the rest of Fitz-Ausculf's lands in this County; and containing one Hide was valued at 20s.'

In the Domesday survey it was written 'Witone', but later appeared as 'Wicton', with a derivation signifying 'a bend in the river'. The name is fairly common, as there are at least ten 'Wittons' in the country. To distinguish it from its namesakes it was sometimes referred to as 'Witton Wood'. During the course of time Witton passed to the crown, and Henry III granted it to one, Andrew, henceforward known as 'Andrew de Wicton'. In 1240 it is recorded that Andrew had a dispute over boundaries with his neighbour at Perry. This was resolved by a jury of twelve Knights of the Shire, who were summoned at the King's command.

Witton has changed hands many times during its recorded history, and the names of two owners of the manor — John Wyrley and George Birch — are perpetuated in the names of roads in the district. It was a scattered community, without the focal point of a village, but although it had no church it had a hall, described as being 'isolated in swampy hollowlands'. The modern Witton Hall, near the junction of Brookvale Road and George Road, is, in all probability, the fourth building to answer to the name, the first two having been moated.

Unfamiliar Witton : stunted and wind-swept trees on the breezy slopes of the 'Bleak Hills'

The Birchfield Road tram terminus early in the present century

Someone once described Witton as ' . . . romantic upland and valley, mingled in strange profusion', and the phrase may at the time have been apt. Certainly the impression of a sombre place, enshrouded in a miasma of fog and factory fumes along the valley of the murky, flood-prone Tame is quickly dispelled on the breezy slopes to the north. The 'Bleak Hills', now largely built up, once had a windmill on their crest. Witton Cemetery commands some expansive views, and until a few years ago the nearby uplands of overgrown allotments, (now built upon), still had a wildness, enhanced by stunted and wind-swept trees, bracken and wiry heathland grass, a reminder that this was once the southern fringe of Sutton Coldfield Chase. A little spring rose nearby, but its pure waters have long since ceased to run, having apparently been diverted underground by sand-boring operations.

At the point where the Roman Icknield Street crossed the River Tame at Perry Barr it is claimed that the legionnaires had a small garrison. Whether this is true we cannot say, nor can we be sure as to the exact spot at which the crossing was made. The name 'Holford', however, suggests a

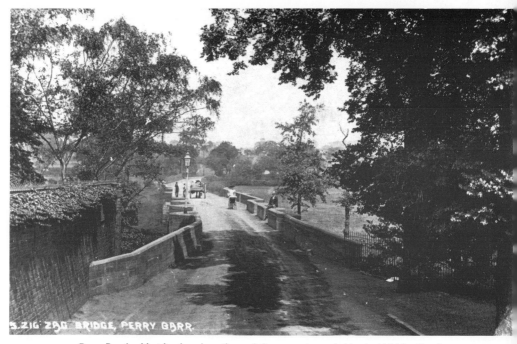

Perry Barr's oldest landmark — the pack-horse or zig-zag bridge in Aldridge Road

69

Perry Common Road, 1925

Kingstanding Road, 1928

corruption of 'old ford', and from its position on the map we can infer that the Romans forded the river a short distance down stream from the present bridges in Aldridge Road. At the time of Domesday, Perry Barr, like Erdington, was rated at three hides. It was held at that time by Drogo, from the Norman overlord, Fitz-Ausculf.

In an early document there is reference to 'a smythie or furnace in Perry barre', and we know that by 1538 there was a forge in existence, with bellows operated by water. This forge, we are told was destroyed by fire and rebuilt in 1597. Possessing fertile land as well as a good water supply, Perry Barr once had several water mills. One of them was used by William Hutton, the 18th century Birmingham historian, for paper-making.

The pack-horse or zig-zag bridge in Aldridge Road is probably the oldest structure in Perry Barr, for although it is said to have been built by Sir Henry Gough, squire of Perry Barr, in 1709 to replace an earlier, wooden bridge, it appears to be considerably older. It certainly bears some similarity to the Vesey Bridge at Water Orton, which was built in the reign of Henry VIII. The parish church is not as old as it looks; its first stone was laid in 1831, the first year of the reign of William IV. Perry Barr then may well have been an idyllic place. Today, although its churchyard is ringed with

Kingstanding Road, 1942

factories, and the once clear waters of the Tame filthy beyond description, its ancient elms destroyed by Dutch elm-disease and its skyline punctuated by high-rise flats and an elevated motorway, yet its tree-fringed cricket-pitch and park beyond, still give it an aura of rusticity.

Kingstanding is a modern community which has built up its own identity in the last half-century. In former times it was a wild region of common-land and a popular venue for prize fighting and cock fighting. Its chief historical feature is the Roman Icknield Street, the course of which passes through Kingstanding. Before the vast building activities of the early 'thirties, there were fields bearing the names 'Roman field' and 'Lower Roman field'. Coins found in these fields included those of the reigns of Domitian, Trajan, Hadrian, Antonius Pius and Marcus Aurelius.

The name of Kingstanding is ascribed to the fact that Charles I addressed local supporters from thereabouts at the beginning of the Civil War in 1642. The exact spot is claimed to be a small mound at the top of the hill in Kingstanding Road, on the left hand side going towards the Parson and Clerk Hotel. Until recently the site had a fence round it. The derivation of the name Kingstanding, however, may not be the obvious one, for according to the Oxford English Dictionary, 'standing' is defined as meaning a hunter's station or stand from which to shoot game', and since the area, so close to Sutton Park, was once part of a Royal Forest, much frequented by ancient kings and renowned for its game, this derivation is not wholly lacking in credibility.

Sir Josiah Mason (left)

A H. Saxton, a local printer, remembered for his book, "Bygone Erdington" (1928)

Some Local Worthies

*A few of the people who have featured in Erdington's
transition from hamlet to thriving suburb.*

Doctor George Bodington was a medical practitioner in Erdington before
moving back to his home town of Sutton Coldfield to care for the mentally
sick and where, later, he became a pioneer in the treatment of pulmonary
consumption.

F. B. Collier. When the railway was built in 1862 there were a great number
of navvies working and living in the district, many of whom were heavy
drinkers. Collier, a Sunday-school teacher, with others, organised crowded
temperance meetings in the Village. He was also associated with a night
school, held two or three times a week, in which many boys and men were
taught to read and write.

George C. Dean was a draper who had his shop beside the Village Green.
He was a member of Erdington UDC. and took an active part in the affairs
of the Village.

Doctor W. Donovan had his practice in the Village. He was a fiery-
tempered Irishman, described as being cultured, generous, witty, genial and
good-hearted. He is remembered as a fighter in the cause of improved
sanitation and lighting in the Village.

Doctor Paget Evans, a member of Erdington UDC., sponsored the building
of Moor End School on the grounds that it was dangerous for children
living on the east side of the Village to have to cross the High Street to get to
the older Osborne Road School.

Henry Flint was a builder who was responsible for developing a number of
roads in Erdington, including Oxford Road, York Road, Johnson Road
and Dean Road. York Road had been a cart-track and upon land beside it,
the Erdington Wakes were held, consisting of shows, roundabouts,
coconut-shies and stalls, to which people came from far and wide.

William Fowler enjoyed the rare distinction of having lived in three
centuries. He died in 1804, aged 107. He was steward of the Aston Hall
estate and built himself a house on a plot of land at Gravelly Hill where five
generations of his family subsequently lived. His granddaughter married
Dr. George Bodington.

Tom Green was Erdington's first appointed postman. Prior to his appointment a man named Isaac Carter acted as postman and was paid two pence for each letter he delivered. He was assisted by a woman named Annie Hart. In 1874 Tom Green took up his duties and four years later was officially appointed postman, with Carter acting as auxiliary. Tom Green survived until September, 1928 when, tragically, at the age of 81, he was burned to death.

John Hingeley was a local historian, antiquary, writer and lecturer and the author of *Erdington Since the Conquest.* He was also an early broadcaster from the local station, known as '5 I.T.'

W.E. Lee was a member of Erdington UDC. and also Chairman of the Tramways Committee, whose dual-role enabled him to overcome much local opposition to the electric tramway, which reached Erdington in 1907.

Sir Josiah Mason, industrialist and philanthropist, built and endowed the Josiah Mason Orphanage (see page 43).

W. Nock established Nock's Brickworks in Holly Lane in 1876, which survived until 1966, when the clay ran out. It was an old-style family business in which five generations of the family were involved.

Thomas Ryland of the Redlands, Gravelly Hill was Chairman of the Rural Sanitary Authority, who played an active part in making various improvements during the early development of the Village. He died in 1905.

Miss Mary Ryland interested herself on behalf of the poor of the parish. She founded the Erdington Charity Organisation, which did much helpful work among the sick and needy.

A. H. Saxton was a printer who founded the firm of A. H. Saxton, (Printers) Ltd. in Summer Road, Erdington. In co-operation with John Hingeley he produced the profusely illustrated *Bygone Erdington* in 1928. The long-established *Saxton's Recorder* was a news booklet, circulated free to householders.

Charles Smith was the first headmaster of Osborne Road School, a post which he held for 35 years.

Sir Benjamin Stone, successful business man, member of parliament for East Birmingham and first Mayor of Sutton Coldfield is remembered for his legacy of thousands of photographs, many of them of great local interest (see page 39).

John Wilton helped in forming the Lighting Board at a time when the only lamp in the parish was on the Village Green. The Board adopted an Act of George IV, (Lighters and Watchers Act), and charged six pence in the pound in places where lamps were erected. Several lamps were erected along the main road at a cost of 22/6d. (£1.12½) each.

Emma Jane Worboise was born in Birmingham in 1825 and lived at Sutton Road, Erdington between 1865 and 1870. She was an author, in whose book, *Overdale,* it is claimed that Victorian Erdington is recognisable. She died at Clevedon in 1887, the widow of a Baptist minister.

Bibliography

The Antiquities of Warwickshire   Sir William Dugdale
                (1656)

Erdington Since the Conquest   J. Hingeley
                (1900)

Bygone Erdington   A.H. Saxton
                (1928)

Victoria History of the Counties of England
                (Vol. 7)

Early Settlement in Erdington   R. Stanley-Morgan
    (A documentary case-study read before the
Birmingham Archaeological Society at their
meeting on 28th January, 1964).

Erdington, Past and Present   Michael J. Arkinstall and
                (1976)   Patrick C. Baird,
                        BA., A.L.A.

Unpublished papers on Erdington.   N. C. Meacham

ERDINGTON ON OLD POSTCARDS

By courtesy of Mr D.A. Spinks and Mr John Marks

Erdington, High Street

Baptist Chapel, Erdington

Erdington. The Village looking towards Sutton.   "Scott" Series No. 610.

High St. Erdington. — 156.

High Street, Erdington

RAILWAY STATION ERDINGTON

A day at the races — Bromford Bridge style

Stockland Green. Tram Terminus.　Ann Series 316.

Sutton Road, Erdington.